D0734531

FILLED WITH *Joy*

A DAILY GUIDEPOSTS PRAYER COMPANION

Guideposts

New York

Filled with Joy: A Daily Guideposts Prayer Companion

Published by Guideposts Books & Inspirational Media
110 William Street
New York, New York 10038
Guideposts.org

Acknowledgments

Every attempt has been made to credit the sources of copyrighted material used in this book. If any such acknowledgment has been inadvertently omitted or miscredited, receipt of such information would be appreciated.

Scripture quotations marked (ESV) are taken from the *Holy Bible, English Standard Version*, copyright © 2001 by Crossway Bibles, a division of Good News Publishers. Used by permission. All rights reserved.

Scripture quotations marked (KJV) are taken from The King James Version of the Bible.

Scripture quotations marked (NAS) are taken from the *New American Standard Bible*, copyright © 1960, 1962, 1963, 1968, 1971, 1972, 1973, 1975, 1977, 1995 by the Lockman Foundation. Used by permission.

Scripture quotations marked (NIV) are taken from *The Holy Bible, New International Version*. Copyright © 1973, 1978, 1984, 2011 by Biblica, Inc. Used by permission of Zondervan. All rights reserved worldwide. www.zondervan.com

Scripture quotations marked (NKJV) are taken from *The Holy Bible, New King James Version*. Copyright © 1982 by Thomas Nelson, Inc.

Scripture quotations marked (NLT) are from the *Holy Bible, New Living Translation*. Copyright© 1996, 2004, 2007 by Tyndale House Foundation. Used by permission of Tyndale House Publishers Inc., Carol Stream, Illinois 60188. All rights reserved.

Scripture quotations marked (NRSV) are taken from the *New Revised Standard Version Bible*. Copyright © 1989 by the Division of Christian Education of the National Council of the Churches of Christ in the United States of America. Used by permission. All rights reserved.

Scripture quotations marked (TLB) are taken from *The Living Bible*. Copyright © 1971 by Tyndale House Publishers, Wheaton, Illinois 60187. All rights reserved.

Cover and interior design by Müllerhaus
Cover photo by Shutterstock
Typeset by Aptara

Printed and bound in the United States of America
10 9 8 7 6 5 4 3 2 1

An Introductory Note

Daily Guideposts writers have always grounded their devotions—whether about love, family, illness, or wisdom—with a closing prayer. We've always believed that prayer represents the closest possible connection to our loving God; it's the way, even through our earthly lives, that God sees into our hearts and knows our soul. This year's *Daily Guideposts* theme is "Filled with Joy," and it's through prayer that we express gratitude and joy to God. We sincerely hope that our prayer companion helps you to develop a more loving relationship with our Creator. Prayer is not a mysterious practice reserved only for clergy or the eloquent. Prayer is simply communicating with God—talking to and waiting patiently to hear and understand God's response. We encourage you to pray from the heart, freely, spontaneously, and in your own words. If you are at a loss for words, perhaps the prayers contained in this volume will guide you on your journey.

Psalm 126:3 (NIV) tells us... "The Lord has done great things for us, and we are filled with joy."

Amen.

A PRAYER FOR AUTUMN. THE AIR IS VERY still, Lord, on this last day of September, and I know what it means. It's that little pause that comes between summer and winter, a pause called autumn.

They say it's "The Melancholy Season," but it's my favorite time of the year. I love the way You transform aging green leaves into bright flowers. It's like a second spring. I savor the short, dreamy days and the crisp nights, lightly scented with burning leaves. I love walking across the leaf-littered lawn—it's like walking on a field of potato chips. A cool breeze caresses my face, and after a hot summer it feels like Your Holy Spirit breathing new life into this old man. At night, I fall asleep to the hypnotic *creak, creak, creak* of the crickets.

Old is where I live now, Lord. I am in the September of my years, with more years behind me than ahead of me. And yet, the perspective is such a relief! Looking back, I can see clearly Your footprints in my past. At the time, my troubles hid Your face from me, but now I can see plainly that You were there all along, weaving even my trials into a rich tapestry of experience.

I wish I could have trusted You more in the past, but I was afraid a lot. Now that I am closer to the end, I am not so afraid anymore, Father.

My heart is as still as a day in September.

—*Daniel Schantz*

FATHER GOD, IT'S MORE THAN I CAN comprehend—how You care about me and love me as You do. It's too wonderful for words. Thank You for Your Son Who made it possible to know You. Thank You for Your Spirit Who reminds me how to follow Your will.

The more I know You, Father, Jesus, and Holy Spirit, the more I want to know You, the deeper, closer relationship I want to have with You. Realizing we can have that relationship, and You want it too, brings me to my knees. Reveal to me, teach me, all I can know of You on this earth. Instruct me in Your will and Your way. Show me how to walk with You more intimately. May I let nothing of this world be a barrier between us.

Even with the blessings You've given me, I know I've only tasted of Your goodness. Feed me with Your bread of life, fill me with Your living water, until the joy of Your presence pours from me onto others.

Let me know You better. Lead me to more fully grasp the beauty of Your love and more thoroughly experience the richness of Your peace. Immerse me in Your Word, increase my understanding, sharpen my awareness. Cleanse me from anything that would divert my heart from You. Bring me to a place of turning to You, talking with You, knowing You, and following You as constantly and completely as in Your power I can.

Amen.

—*Kim Henry*

DEAR FATHER, YOU'VE SHOWERED MY days with blessings, and I've been slow to say thank You. I remember to tell You *WOW* when a prayer is answered but I forget to tell You *THANKS* for the rain, the ice cream cones, the smiles, the chats with dear friends, all the little treats in my day. So today I am remembering to say thank You, dear Father, for Your kind care.

Amen.

—*Lisa Bogart*

THANK YOU, LORD, FOR MY CIRCLE OF friends. We've shared happy family times, career achievements, and financial successes. We've also upheld each other through devastating losses, serious illnesses, family upheavals, and belt-tightening poverty. So often, Jesus, the faces of my friends have been Your face, and their words have echoed Your words. My friends have rejoiced with me and wept with me. Their prayers have gladdened my heart and eased my burdens, as I hope my prayers have done for them. I praise You, gracious God, for this precious gift of friendship.

—*Penney Schwab*

FATHER GOD, YOU ARE SOVEREIGN AND good. Thank You for Your character that never changes. I'm so grateful that the truth of Who You are does not depend on anything—not my feelings, not on the opinions of others, and not on my circumstances. Help me cling to You today, knowing that You are a strong tower, a sun and a shield, and a place of refuge.

—*Katie Ganshert*

OH, MIGHTY GOD! I LONG TO HAVE OTHERS see my love for You in every part of me: my physical being, my words, my thoughts, my acts. Let Your light shine through me, God! Make me a reflection, however dim, of the joy that comes in communing with You. Let my joy be so full that it spills over as a light unto others.

Amen.

—*Marci Alborghetti*

As I work each day to raise my child to follow You, help me to remember to make the most of each moment as it comes. There are lessons in church and intentional time, but also lessons in waiting in line at the grocery store, getting caught in a rainstorm, or having our plans canceled at the last minute. As I help her grow, help me remember that my example is far more powerful than my words.

—*Ashley Kappel*

FATHER, HOW GRATEFUL I AM FOR THE way You set me free. I confess to holding on to bitterness and resentment, but You showed me the choice to forgive that was mine. When I decided once and for all to forgive, I was able to fly with the freedom of a bird. Thank You, Lord, for the swiftness of my steps, the joy in my heart, and the peace for my nights. Because of Your power in me to forgive, I am now a reflection of Your love that glows with gratitude, for You have set me free. In Jesus's name, I thank You.

—*Janet Perez Eckles*

FOR DIRTY DISHES,

For congealing leftovers,

For messy abundance,

We bless You, Lord.

—Gail Thorell Schilling

HEAVENLY FATHER,

Teach me today to accept Your acceptance of me.

When the drive to prove myself nags at me again and again, let me feel Your never-failing approval. When I doubt my capabilities, let me sense Your enabling hand and revel in the gifts You've placed in me. When I fear what tomorrow may bring, let me remember that You have seen all my tomorrows and are already there. When I look in the mirror and don't like what I see, let me know Your boundless love, just as I am, without one change.

Your Son, Jesus, is precious to You beyond description. Let me take my place, at His side, as one of the blood-bought children of God, loved beyond compare. Teach me today to accept Your acceptance of me, and to accept those around me in the very same way.

Through Christ I pray.

Amen.

—*Bill Giovannetti*

HEAVENLY FATHER, I KNOW I OFTEN GET bogged down in my prayers—asking, asking, asking. I come to You every time I want something, even if it's a prayer for a sick friend or a need for a frazzled family member. Mostly it's needs that I have. But today, I just want to say thank You, Lord. Thank You for this day, this glorious day. Thank You for things in Your creation that fill me with simple joy. The sky. Such a color of blue, Lord. How do You do that? Thank You for the sun, the breeze, the lovely temperature. My skin feels good when I step into Your world, Lord. Thank You. Thank You for this wonderful spring day and how it makes me feel joyful. Thank You.

—*Patty Kirk*

WHEN I AM DISAPPOINTED IN MYSELF, or feeling too small or too used up to serve any purpose, Lord, help me to see myself as You see me. You see orphans as queens and abandoned sons as kings. Help me to see the light that You have placed inside of me, and give me the courage to be all You've made me to be!

—*Sharon Foster*

FATHER, THANK YOU FOR PSALM 121:1
(NRSV). I need it today. You tell us, "I lift
up my eyes to the hills—from where will
my help come?" When I'm tempted to run
to people for my answers, I'm searching
in the wrong direction. All I need to do
is to lift my eyes toward You. You are my
Helper.

—*Julie Garmon*

GOOD MORNING, LORD. THANK YOU FOR gifting me with a brand-new day, clean and bright. Give me the courage to release the past and start afresh at this very moment. With Your forgiveness, create in me a clean heart by releasing me from the debt of my sins. With Your love, gently guide me to Your truth. And with Your grace, reveal to me how to become a person who reflects Who You are so that when the people around me look at me—they see You in me. In Your name.

Amen.

—*Rebecca Ondov*

LORD, THERE ARE SO MANY MYSTERIES in life—things I don't understand. But the biggest question is: Why do You care so much about each one of us. The same omnipotent God, Who spoke the universe into creation with His words, is accessible to me at any time, day or night. The God of history and eternity wants to hear often from me through prayer. Your wish is to have fellowship with mankind...to walk with me as I go through my mundane days and nights. It blows my mind that You, dear God, desire a relationship with me in this very moment. Imagine!

—*Stephanie Thompson*

I am speechless over Your heavens, majestic Creator! From this mountain deck tonight the stars crowd out the sky. The Big Dipper sits on the ridge like You laid it down. The psalmist sings of day and night—without voice–uttering knowledge across the earth (Psalm 19:2–4). I hear the shout. You are God, great and mighty! Beautiful in power! And I, who can usually find things to say, am silent.

—*Carol Knapp*

LORD, YOU'VE ALLOWED THIS DIFFICULT season in my life. Remind me in my times of struggle, sadness, and frustration that this indeed is a season. It will have its end. Let this season not consume me or deceive my spirit into hopelessness, but instead sharpen and teach me; strengthen and use me for Your glory. Speak to my heart, encourage me, Lord. Walk with me through these days as I journey into a new season, a new morning, a new appreciation for the life You've given me.

—*Karen Valentin*

DEAR FATHER, I NEED TO GET AWAY from all of the stressful noise in my life. My ears need a break from all of the opinions, demands, and chatter. I find it hard to think and hard to pray with so much noise going on both outside of me and inside of me. Help me to unplug from the words of somebody else's song so I will have a chance to hear the sweet, still melody of the song of peace and calmness that You are composing in my soul. Teach me to crave silence and to seek it until I find it at some forgotten hour in some sheltered corner of my world. Give me joy and rest in those precious moments of stillness spent in Your nurturing presence.

Amen.

—*Karen Barber*

Today, You gave me air to fill my lungs, water to quench my thirst, food to ease my hunger, and Your love to surround me. Thank You, God, for another good day.

—*Rhoda Blecker*

THIS MORNING AS I GAZE OUTSIDE MY cabin window, there is just a sliver of sun in the sky. I think of the verse in Your Word, Psalm 118:24 (KJV): "This is the day the Lord hath made; we will rejoice and be glad in it." Thank You for the gift of a brand-new day. What can I do with this day, Lord, this moment?

—*Roberta Messner*

A BIRTHDAY PRAYER: THANK YOU, Father, for the gift of the past twelve months! I cannot add a single day, not as much as a minute, to my life, but You have sustained me, nourished me, protected me for another year. Let me use today to review those months. To think with gratitude of all those on whose love, or skill, or labor I have depended. To ask forgiveness for my want of charity, and the many times I've fallen short of Your will for me. Help me to walk closer to You in the new year opening before me.

—*Elizabeth Sherrill*

A PRAYER FOR WINTER. FORGIVE ME, Father, but I am not overly fond of winter and sometimes wonder why You made it. I need warm weather to do the things I love: gardening . . . biking . . . fishing. Even my prayers are better, offered under a starry, summer sky. In winter, You take away my toys and send me to my room, like I am being punished.

And yet, Lord, I can see Your wisdom in winter. It's a kind of Sabbath, isn't it? You force me to slow down so that I will last longer. In summer I work and play so hard that my joints are throbbing by October, and my skin is leathery from the hot sun. But by spring, my joints are flexible and my face is smooth. In the summer my brain gets lazy from disuse, but in the wintertime I rediscover books and conversation.

I hate to admit it, Lord, but winter can be useful. The cold air forces me indoors where I can enjoy cozy fellowship with my family, around the fireplace. The white snow reminds me of Your grace, which cleanses me of my sins. Your stars are glorious on a cold, December night, and the darkest time of the year is the perfect time for a huge party, like Christmas.

And so, Lord, reluctantly, grudgingly, I thank You for winter. But please, God, couldn't You make it just a little bit shorter?

—*Daniel Schantz*

HELLO, MY FATHER IN HEAVEN. AS YOU know, I'm getting ready to step outdoors and take a walk. I'm trying to do that every day, Lord, because I know I need the exercise and stepping into Your world forces me to smile and say hi to my neighbors, allows me to breathe in fresh air and smell the flowers, and become a part of the world around me. I need to be out there, Lord, because it renews my faith, helps me appreciate my surroundings, exercises my body, causes me to use my brain to think of all sorts of things while I'm walking and, most of all, gives me time to say my prayers. So Lord, here I go, putting on my jacket, ready for some You-and-me time.

—*Patty Kirk*

DEAR LORD, I HAVE A DECISION TO MAKE and I need Your help. What I choose to do will affect me and others in ways I can imagine and in ways I cannot foresee. I'm scared, Lord. Scared of making a choice I'll regret, of doing the wrong thing.

I don't know the future. You do. I don't know which path I should take. You do. Give me wisdom to make the best choice, the one that is Your will for my life.

In Your Word You tell me not to fret or worry. I confess that's what I've been doing. I want to stop. So right now I turn this decision over to You, Lord. Lead me. Guide me. Help me know what You want me to do. Give me patience to listen for, and discernment to recognize, Your voice in my heart. Let me not mistake Your voice for my own, telling me what I think I want to hear. Take the turmoil I'm feeling and turn it into the peace of knowing my decision and its outcome are in Your hands. Grant me the calm that comes when the choice I make is in Your will.

Thank You for caring, Lord.

Amen.

—Kim Henry

DEAR FATHER, I AM RUSHING. ERRANDS are mounting. Chores are pressing. The details of life are looming. I am racing from one task to the next. Slow me down today. Give me the calm to know I have just the right amount of time to do Your work. Remind me of what's truly important and help me to concentrate my efforts there.

Amen.

—*Lisa Bogart*

TODAY IT SEEMS LIKE I'M MAJORING IN minors. In my mind, little slights become neglect; traffic delays are designed just to upset my schedule; and a casual word is somehow changed into an insult. Help me turn my thought-life around, Lord! Let me deliberately think about "what is true and good . . . and dwell on the fine, good things in others" (Philippians 4:8, TLB). And thank You for the peace and joy that come when I focus on You.

—*Penney Schwab*

HELP ME TO REMEMBER THE IMPORTANCE of friendship, God. Days float by and my to-do list grows and I'm seeing friends fall by the wayside. You call us to fellowship and community; remind me that time spent with friends is not time squandered, but rather time that results in a full heart and a renewed sense of joy.

—*Ashley Kappel*

FATHER, YOU HAVE GIVEN ME SO MUCH! I rejoice in the abundance of Your presence and the prosperity You've given me, knowing full well that I provide nothing on my own, and that everything I have, and am, comes from You. Though I may not have what others call great wealth, it is great to me for it is all Your gift. Help me, Father, to follow Your laws and to be free with what You have given me so that others can share my joy and experience more completely Your gifts to me and to them. Let my generosity be a demonstration of Your abiding love for all people.

Amen.

—*Marci Alborghetti*

LORD, SOMETIMES I AM ALL TOO QUICK to speak and all too quick to become angry. Forgive me for these sins. I don't want to be this way. Please, God, put a guard over my mouth today. When angry, bitter, unkind, or impatient words bubble up inside me, help me to keep quiet and lay them before You in repentance. May the words from my mouth be pleasing to You today and always. Be glorified in my speech. Let my words be a welcome, sweet offering.

—*Katie Ganshert*

FATHER, CHANGE MY HEART TO KNOW contentment. Restore in me a heart to appreciate what You gave me, where You put me, and where You're taking me. Grant me a heart of gratitude—to accept Your will, to relish in Your power, and to rely on the depth of Your love. All my tomorrows are in Your hands. And till the day when You bring about a change, grant me the patience that turns to peace, ushers in contentment, and calms my soul. In Jesus's name.

Amen.

—*Janet Perez Eckles*

I approach Your throne of grace, this day, God, not to ask—You know I do plenty of that—but to praise. I praise You for the shoes on my feet. I praise You for the pillow beneath my head last night. I praise You for the breath in my lungs, the shirt on my back, and whatever wits remain in my brain.

Thank You for the many bounties I've taken for granted. Thank You for those who have been kind to me. Thank You for those who have taught me, prayed for me, put up with me, hugged me, encouraged me, and, yes, corrected me when I've strayed. I even thank You for the hard times, the losses, and the pains. I don't understand them, but I'm grateful for Your hand in every dark valley.

Thank You for the Bible and Your precious wisdom there. Thank You for Jesus, the Lamb of God, my Redeemer, and my Friend. Thank You for that glorious land beyond life's veil, where I shall one day open my eyes and breathe celestial air, and see my Savior face-to-face.

I'm not asking today, Lord. I'm praising. And I'm thanking. And I'm declaring that You've been better to me than I've ever deserved.

Amen.

—*Bill Giovannetti*

LORD, AS I LAY MY NEEDS BEFORE YOU, my heart reminds me that there are so many people who have no shelter and no food. I am grateful for what You provide for me and for those I love. Help me to be mindful of those who are in need. Lord, bless the poor and show me ways I can serve and help.

—*Sharon Foster*

FATHER, PSALM 139:5 (NLT) TELLS ME, "You go before me and follow me." What a wonderful truth. No matter where I go— whether it's into surgery or on vacation— You're with me. I can simply whisper Your name, and You're already there.

—*Julie Garmon*

IT'S SUCH A LONG LIST OF COURAGEOUS acts, Lord. All the great heroes of faith in Hebrews 11. I feel small beside them. Until that one little spot (verse 34, NAS) that says they "from weakness were made strong." There have been those times I wanted to give up...didn't think I could do it...was too afraid...too discouraged. I called to You—and You took what was weak in me, like a blacksmith at the forge, and fashioned something strong. Just like You did for those on the list.

—*Carol Knapp*

THERE'S SOMETHING MAGICAL ABOUT morning. Not the mornings when I hit the snooze bar, hoping for seven more minutes before stumbling out of bed, but those mornings when I'm awakened ever so gently from sleep. As I lay in the stillness, random thoughts course through my mind. It's in the darkness that the New Testament says Jesus met You, God, for prayer. Before the duties and distractions of the day closed in, the Son of God sought His Father. Rather than rolling over, I can claim the magic of the morning too, alone with You.

—*Stephanie Thompson*

ON THE DAYS WHEN I FEEL RICKETY, worn down, and as if there are gaping holes in my heart, Lord, I ask that You send the mighty rushing wind of the Holy Spirit to fill me up. Strengthen my inner self with Your power and refresh me with Your living waters. In Your name.

Amen.

—*Rebecca Ondov*

FATHER, I AM FAR FROM HOME,

Staying in a place I've never been before.

All around me are strangers' faces.

Some smile as I pass, but they are smiles of courtesy,

Not recognition. Not the glad greeting of friendship.

The welcome in stores and restaurants is professional.

Not personal.

So, tonight I am feeling lonely.

When I take my loneliness to You, Father,

... You fill my heart with gratitude

For the welcome and the smiles,

However perfunctory.

Your Son was not always welcomed.

Common courtesy was denied Him in the Pharisee's house.

…You prick my heart with shame for my self-centeredness.

Your Son was often on unfamiliar roads.

He loved the strangers He met there.

…You warm my heart when You ask:

How can You say that You are far from home?

In Me You live and move and have Your being.

There is nowhere You can be where I am not,

No place so far that my love does not reach.

Welcome home, my daughter. Rest tonight in Me.

—Elizabeth Sherrill

SOMEONE I BELIEVED WAS MY FRIEND said something unkind and untrue about me. It's the latest scuttlebutt at work. But I read in Your Word this morning that no one can really hurt me because I have Your protection. Hebrews 13:6 (NKJV) says, "The Lord is my helper, I will not fear. What can man do to me?" I will believe those words, Lord. Today, and every day.

—*Roberta Messner*

GOOD MORNING, GOD. IF I DO THINGS right today, help me not to think that I did them alone. If I make mistakes today, help me not to think that they mean I'm stupid. If I can't figure out whether something is right or a mistake, please show me where to find some wisdom, because I'm going to need it!

—*Rhoda Blecker*

FATHER, I NEED YOUR GUIDANCE TODAY. I have sought the counsel of Your Word in the Bible. And yet I do not want to go forward until I have brought my decision before You in prayer. I seek Your peace upon my heart and mind that I am doing the right thing. If this is not the right thing for me, I pray that You make me restless and unsure until I have prayed it through and found Your peace. Help me not to lean on my own understanding, but to wait until You direct my path (Proverbs 3:5, 6).

Amen.

—*Karen Barber*

I HAVE LOTS OF RESPONSIBILITIES IN MY life, Lord. Many things lay solely on my shoulders. At times, these burdens are heavy and I treat them as a curse. I need to adjust my thinking. Thank You, Lord, for my piles of laundry; my kids and I have plenty of clothes to wear. Thank You for my sink full of dirty dishes. It means I was able to feed my family to their hearts' content. Thank You for a home that is mine to clean. Thank You for my bills. You've allowed me the provisions to pay them, and each one represents a service I was blessed to receive. Thank You for my job. It provides for my family, and the people I work with have truly become a part of my extended family. And most of all, thank You for my children. The love and the joy they give me will forever outweigh the challenges of being their mom. Without them, I would be well rested, but I wouldn't have such an important reason to work so hard.

—*Karen Valentin*

SUDDENLY, IT'S SUMMER, LORD! No more late frost warnings or chilly nights. The ground is as warm as a fresh-baked biscuit. When I awake in the morning, it's light outside. The kitchen windows are open, the curtains are blowing, and I can see my wife hanging clothes on the line. I'm wearing a T-shirt, and my arms are naked. I can hear the neighbors' children playing kickball in the street, and their parents mowing their lawns.

And yet, it's already too hot, and it's only June. I think of my mother's old saying: "As a rule, man's a fool, when it's hot he wants it cool; When it's cool, he wants it hot; Always wanting what is not."

Someday it will be perfect, God, You promised. You said that in heaven it's always summer, but it's never too hot. It's the best of all worlds up there. Picnics without ants. Eating without gaining weight. Friendships without hurt feelings. Playing hard, but never tired.

When I get to heaven, Lord, I am going to break into a run and run for seven days straight. I haven't been able to run for years. I'm going to swim in the River of Life that flows from the throne. I'm going to sample every fruit on the Tree of Life.

Sometimes I think summer will never get here, Lord. But just when I think it's never going to happen, then suddenly, it's heaven!

—*Daniel Schantz*

I'm doing it again, Lord, fighting the facts. I don't like what's happened. I'm disappointed, angry, and upset. This is not the way I wanted things to be. I've done my best but it's made no difference. I'm facing something that's hard to accept. I feel like screaming, "It's not fair!"

Quiet my heart and spirit, Lord. Still my mental thrashing. Help me to breathe deeply of Your love, to find rest in Your arms.

Remind me You and You alone are God, that I am not. You are in control. You know what's best. Your Word tells me Your ways are not my ways, Your thoughts are not my thoughts. You've also said no eye has seen nor mind conceived what You have in store for those who love You. I love

You, Lord. I just don't love what I'm going through. Bring me the peace of knowing You'll use it for good.

Help me accept what is. Show me where to go from here. May I use my energy to move forward instead of trying to change the past. Guide me along this difficult path. May I experience the joy of reaching its destination, having held Your hand every step of the way.

Amen.

—Kim Henry

DEAR FATHER, TECHNOLOGY GETS THE better of me. The temptation to surf the Web, veg out with TV, or fiddle with my phone is very strong. I feel pulled in many directions when I am sitting in front of a screen. Lift my head. Raise my eyes to the sky. Remind me there is a world You have made where I can engage with real people. Give me a rest from screens today!

Amen.

—Lisa Bogart

HERE I AM AGAIN, LORD, ASKING forgiveness for gossiping—the same sin I committed yesterday and last week. I didn't say anything that wasn't true, but the truth reflected poorly on someone. Maybe there were reasons for her actions. Regardless, I should have kept my mouth shut. James says, "If anyone can control his tongue, it proves he has perfect control over himself in every other way" (3:1, TLB). My own words convict me and show just how far I am from perfect control! Forgive me, Lord. Help me rely on Your grace to speak words that are helpful, never hurtful.

—*Penney Schwab*

LORD, THANK YOU FOR COMING TO earth and being our example. You were all about the least of these. I pray today that You will open my eyes to the hurting, the lost, the overlooked. Forgive me for holding on to my comfort and conveniences. Forgive me for being wrapped up in my problems and my to-do lists. Break my heart for what breaks Yours. Let me see with Your eyes. I pray for a willing, humble spirit. In Your name,

Amen.

—*Katie Ganshert*

JESUS, WHEN I DISCOVER YOU IN unexpected places, I feel a joy that must be akin to that of the wise men upon finding You, the King of the Jews, the King of the World, as a tiny babe in a stable, the most humble of dwellings. But why should I be surprised when You are always discovered in the most unlikely places, dear Jesus? My joy is multiplied when I consider where You can be found: among the poor, the sick, the downtrodden; with the addicted, the fearful, the imprisoned; in the field, the church, the institution. Everywhere You went in Your life, You can be found in mine; thus every day provides reason to rejoice.

Amen.

—*Marci Alborghetti*

I AM ABOUT TO TAKE A TRIP, HEAVENLY
Father, and I need Your help to keep me
organized, bring good weather, and guide
and calm the airport personnel, the pilots,
flight attendants. Bless the plane and keep
it safe. Help me to calm the nerves of anyone I see today who is stressed beyond
measure. Help me to find joy and energy
at my destination and to be someone others want to spend time with. Thank You
for this opportunity, Lord, to see a differ-
ent part of Your world and to remember
each adventure during this trip.

—*Patty Kirk*

WHEN THE ANNIVERSARY OF A LOVED one's birth or death comes around, help me to remember the good things from their lives. Often I pause to remember someone on the anniversary of the date of his or her passing, but help me also to remember— and celebrate—on the anniversary of the date of his or her birth. We are more than moments to one another, and our lives should be celebrated with memories, belly laughs, and "Do you remember when" stories, best when shared with other loved ones who are still with us.

—*Ashley Kappel*

FATHER, YOU KNOW THE HURT THAT cruel and unfair words can have on my heart. How often I allowed them to discourage me and echo gloom in my days. But I now know that the words that You call me—Your child, Your beloved, Your creation—the words You use to describe me are the ones that need to resonate in my ears. They will silence messages that do not align with Your Word. I thank You for giving me the wisdom to discern between receiving harsh words or the true, Holy Words that come from You. My ears and heart shall be attentive to the power of Your message and the sweetness of Your affirmation. In Jesus's name, amen.

—*Janet Perez Eckles*

I LAY MY DISAPPOINTMENT AT THE FOOT of the Cross. I am puzzled by Your ways. Truth be told, I'm a bit mad at You. Why did You let me down? Why did You ignore my prayer? Where were You when I needed You most?

Oh, Lord, deep inside, I know better. I know You are good. I know You are faithful. I know You are holy, and perfect.

Still, I ache. So I bring my ache, my pain, my loss, my disappointment to the foot of the Cross. I lay it all there. And when I see Jesus, there, suffering for me, I can't help but know You understand. You never stood aloof from my sorrows and pain. But You plunged into them more deeply than I know.

I see the tapestry of my life from the underside now. It's a jumble of threads, random and absurd. But one day, I'll see the top. I will gasp in wonder at its beauty and grace, and declare I wouldn't change a thing. Until then, dear God, I lay my disappointment at the foot of the Cross, and trust in the love You showed to me there.

In my Savior's love, amen.

—*Bill Giovannetti*

I AM SO GRATEFUL FOR THE BEAUTY around me, God. It is a joy to breathe in Your sweet air and to see blue, or even gray, skies. What a wonder it is, and I feel joy and hope gripping my heart. What a reassurance it is, of how You care for me, of how You care for each one of us.

—*Sharon Foster*

LORD, FORGIVE ME. MY ATTITUDE IS rotten. This project isn't going the way I expected. To be perfectly honest, I'm disappointed. I'm discouraged. I'm tired of trying. But deep in my heart, I know You don't send disappointment and discouragement. You send hope. And strength. And You promise me in Philippians 4:13 (NKJV), "I can do all things through Christ who strengthens me." *All things.*

—*Julie Garmon*

LORD, AS I GO THROUGH MY DAY TODAY, help me to look outside of myself at those around me. Let me see each person I encounter through Your eyes. From the clerk at the store and the one who sweeps the floors to the bustling executives in their suits, help me to remember that You lovingly created every person in Your image. Reveal to me ways that I can share Your love with each one through a thoughtful word, an act of kindness, or perhaps simply a smile. In Your name, amen.

—*Rebecca Ondov*

I'LL ADMIT IT, GOD: I LIKE TO BE FIRST. First in line. First to share my ideas. First to be served at the dinner table. Being first makes me feel good—favored. But being first brings only a temporary feeling of satisfaction. To have true joy, I must rearrange my thinking. As I learned in youth group decades ago, JOY is an acronym. True joy is achieved by putting Jesus first, Others second and yourself last. I must move You and other people to the head of the line, God, if I want to experience joy. Help me to understand that this sort of self-sacrifice is not thinking less of myself, but merely thinking of myself less often.

—*Stephanie Thompson*

WHEN THE PIECES OF MY LIFE SEEM hopelessly scattered, I remember, Jesus, how You told Your disciples when You fed the five thousand with five barley loaves to "gather up the leftover fragments so that nothing will be lost" (John 6:12, NAS). Gather my fragments, my Friend who loves me beyond measure, and make a miracle with them.

—*Carol Knapp*

LORD, THERE'S SUCH A DRIVE INSIDE ME to get everything done! There's always something else to add to my list and it frustrates me when I can't do it all. But it comforts me to know that You're not as worried about it as I am. You don't care if I make a home-cooked meal, or that all the sheets are washed. You're just happy to be with me. And You love it when I set my list aside and just sit with You, my Lord. You said in Your Word, Father, that this is the better choice. Help me to do that more often and forgive me for adding You to the bottom of my to-dos. Let me never forget that I'm more important to You and You're more important to me than my list—any list.

—*Karen Valentin*

DEAR FATHER, TODAY I'M NOT FEELING very confident. When I look at others, they seem so much more self-assured and competent and courageous and strong. In comparison I feel I lack the skills and abilities to meet the challenges I face. I now claim the strong promise You gave St. Paul, "My grace is sufficient for You, for my power is made perfect in weakness" (2 Corinthians 12:9, NIV). And so, Father, today I claim confidence for although I am weak, You are strong. Your strength is more than sufficient for anything You call on me to do. So I joyfully begin this day, confident not in my own strength but in Yours alone.

Amen.

—*Karen Barber*

DEAR LORD, GUIDE ME TO BELIEVE FULLY in the sun when it is concealed behind the clouds, the earth when it is covered in asphalt, the rainbow before the rain ends, and You in every living thing. Even if You seem hidden, let me always believe that You are there.

—*Rhoda Blecker*

THANK YOU FOR THIS CHANCE TO
travel, Father!

To see more of Your world,
Meet more of Your people.
In my excitement over this trip,
Do not let me forget those on journeys
they did not choose.
I am traveling by design.
I leave my home confident of returning.
How many millions upon millions today
are on the road, with no home to return to?
The exiles, the refugees, the dispossessed
by war, or famine, or racial hatred, or religious intolerance.
How many are unwanted in their new
location, without the food and shelter that
a little piece of plastic will secure for me
wherever I go?

Let the homeless wanderers know Your Son's compassion for the outcasts, Father, through Your church's ministries throughout the world, and make me generous in support.

Let me set aside a percentage of my travel budget for those who have no choice but to roam.

—*Elizabeth Sherrill*

FATHER, I AM OVERWHELMED TODAY with a to-do list that stretches the length of my arm. I can't even think straight. So right at this moment I am sitting down with a cup of tea, putting up my feet, taking a deep breath, closing my eyes, and I am going to think of all the ways You have put joy in my life. My husband, children, grandchildren, friends, neighbors, coworkers, church family, home, career, fun activities. I could sit here for hours, Lord, and ponder each one of those categories that You have blessed me with. Thank You. Thank You for blessing me with such a full life. My eyes are open now, Lord, and I am ready to tackle my to-do list. Thank You for this reprieve and especially for all my blessings.

—*Patty Kirk*

My body's tired, Lord, letting me know it's time for sleep. But my mind isn't listening. It's still running full speed ahead. Save me from another night where my thoughts won't turn off and I lie awake wrestling with concerns, issues, problems. Let me not waste this much-needed time for my body and mind to take a break, become restored, and awake refreshed. Free me to sleep deeply. Still my mind, quiet my soul, whisper Your love to my heart. Ensure that I close my eyes and thoughts to the world and sleep, filled with the peace of knowing You.

—*Kim Henry*

THANK YOU, JESUS, FOR MOMENTS OF pure joy that come into my life,

Getting a big hug from my teenage granddaughter,

Rejoicing when a friend is cancer-free for the third straight year,

Sitting with my husband in front of a blazing fire on a subzero night,

Shedding tears of gratitude when I take the bread and wine on Sunday,

For these times and countless others, I am deeply, joyfully, thankful.

—*Penney Schwab*

FATHER GOD, I DESIRE TO LIVE WHOLLY present. With my cell phone at my fingertips, the pull of social media, and the fast pace of this world, it's all too easy to let distractions rule my day. It's all too easy for weeks to pass by in one giant and unfocused blur. God, forgive me for this. Help me to be wholly present with the people You have put in my path and wholly present with whatever tasks You set before me. Let me be present today, Lord, for Your glory and my joy.

—*Katie Ganshert*

COMPASSIONATE FATHER, YOU OFFER ME occasions for both loud joy and quiet joy, and it is often in the quiet times that I feel most keenly Your presence. Where would I be without You, Lord? Where would I be without Your love, protection, refuge? How would I live without Your mercy, forgiveness, redemption, salvation? How would I manage without Your consolation, guidance, succor? I am nothing without You, Lord, and that alone is reason to rejoice. Quietly and loudly.

Amen.

—*Marci Alborghetti*

FATHER, KEEP ME FROM JUMPING AHEAD of You. Grant me the wisdom to wait upon You so I may recognize those choices that follow Your instructions. Keep me from taking steps in the path that will mean disappointment or pain. I count on Your guidance to lead me in the path where the answers will be clear, the results pleasant, and the outcome rewarding. In Jesus's name, amen.

—*Janet Perez Eckles*

MY FATHER, WHO ART IN HEAVEN,

I hallow Your name—I declare You to be God above all, the great I Am, with no one beside You or like You.

Let Your kingdom come, let Your will be done, on earth, as it is in heaven—let the righteousness and joy and peace of heaven be put on display today in my life, my family, my home, my work, my recreation, and in all that I do on earth.

Grant me, I pray, my daily bread—I turn to You as my perfect provision for all I need today. Grant wisdom for my encounters, peace for my struggles, finances for my bills, love for my friends, patience with my enemies, strength for my body, and dedication for my mission to spread Your grace to all I see today.

And forgive me, Lord, even as I forgive those who hurt me—I preset my heart to forgive today. I will not hold grudges. I will let go of bitterness. I will turn from revenge. Let me bask in Your forgiveness of me through Christ's old rugged Cross.

Please lead me not into temptation, but deliver me from all the powers of darkness and evil—though, by Your grace, I can handle my troubles, I pray against those troubles, and ask You to ward them off. Lead me in peace today. Lead me in love. Let my paths be paths of joy and grace.

For Yours is the kingdom and the power and the glory, forever—You are on Your throne, and there is all the confidence I need to face this day and all my tomorrows, forever and ever.

Amen.

—*Bill Giovannetti*

IT IS SO WONDERFUL, LORD, TO SEE YOU bless Your faithful servants. I look at how You are blessing others and I am overcome, weeping with joy! Their blessings, in my heart, feel like my own. Thank You, Lord, for being faithful!

—*Sharon Foster*

LORD, IT'S ME AGAIN. SOMETIMES I wonder if I wear You out when I come to You so often. I'm afraid You've had enough of me, but I'm battling fear again. Still, I'm going to believe Your Word. You tell me in 1 John 4:18 that perfect love casts out all fear. Your love is perfect. Thank You. I'm opening my fingers right now and giving You every speck of fear.

—*Julie Garmon*

GOOD MORNING, LORD. TODAY I WANT to see the beauty of the world through Your eyes. Help me to shut out the clamoring noises, the destruction, and the evil that is all around me. Release me from the cocoon of my concerns. Let me be captured by the beauty of nature, knowing that Your hands fashioned it all for us to enjoy—every plant, every rock, every cloud in the deep blue sky. Let the sunshine warm my heart with Your love. And let the songs of the birds remind me to live a life of praise that will exalt Who You are. In Your name, amen.

—*Rebecca Ondov*

COMMEMORATING HOLIDAYS AND birthdays are what I naturally do. But, Lord, each day that I've been given is a gift from You. Each day holds promise, possibility, and surprises. This is cause to celebrate. By waiting for the major accomplishments or milestones, I'm missing opportunities to rejoice every day. Like the Mad Hatter in *Alice in Wonderland* I could have "a very merry unbirthday party" 364 days a year. Help me to celebrate daily!

—*Stephanie Thompson*

BLESS YOU, MY SAVIOR, FOR TEACHING me not to confuse narrow with confining when You say "the way is narrow that leads to life" (Matthew 7:14). I am journeying this path, though we both know You've reset my steps more than once—and I've got to tell You, I could not have imagined how narrow opens to such awesome glory-filled vistas!

—*Carol Knapp*

THERE'S SO MUCH YOU'RE ASKING ME TO let go of, Lord. My family and dreams are clutched in my arms. On my shoulders, responsibilities and pride. Anger, worries, and memories weigh on my mind. You tell me to let them go. It's not easy to do, but help me to release them and hold on only to You.

—*Karen Valentin*

MY SIMPLEST BLESSING TODAY AND
many other days has been warm fur, a wag-
ging tail, and a cold, wet nose. Thank You,
God, for the companionship of my dog,
who helps me through the toughest times.

—*Rhoda Blecker*

JESUS, I'M FEELING CRITICAL OF SOMEONE right now. I don't think that this person is behaving properly or treating others properly. This person is being unkind, ungrateful, and unfair. You know the things that this person is doing are the things that disturb me the most. My feelings make me want to straighten out this person. So I am bringing my critical thoughts to You. In the light of Your love, kindness, and mercy illuminate my thoughts. As You illuminate them, I realize that You will also illuminate the things in me that are missing the mark of being the person You want me to be. I recall that You told a group of self-righteous people who wanted to straighten out a woman caught in adultery, "Let any one of You who is without sin be the first to throw a stone at her" (John 8:7, NIV). And so, dear Jesus, let me drop this stone of criticism from my hand and instead allow You in Your wisdom and mercy to confront this person. I know that You will deal with this individual in a way that I could never begin to fathom. I pray this person, complete with faults, into Your hands and out of mine.

Amen.

—*Karen Barber*

HELP ME LIVE THE FRUITS OF YOUR Spirit, Lord.

Strengthen me to love even those who seem unlovable.

Fill me so full of the joy of knowing You that it spills out onto those I'm with.

Give me such peace that others are calmed by my presence in the way I'm calmed by Yours.

Breathe patience into me when the wait seems unbearable.

Teach me to be kind even when my kindness is not returned.

Help me remain good in this world where temptation abounds.

Preserve my faithfulness when I want to give up.

Transform my harshness into gentleness of word and action.

Grant me self-control to overcome my sinful nature.

In the heat of the moment, in the midst of the everyday, may Your power enable me to live these fruits, Lord, fruits that will demonstrate I am Your child.

Amen.

—*Kim Henry*

DEAR FATHER, I HAVE WORK TO DO THAT keeps me busy and happy. Remind me that You are in that work as well. When I have the opportunity to give good customer service at my job, let Your light shine through me. When I have the opportunity to write about You in my life, let me do so boldly. Wherever there is a chance to join You in work, let me do so with joy.

Amen.

—Lisa Bogart

BEFORE I FALL ASLEEP, HEAVENLY Father, I want to thank You for this ordinary day. My week has been filled with small but troubling problems and demands on my time. Today nothing happened, and it feels so good! For the moment my little world is at peace and I look forward to a refreshing night's rest. From the bottom of my heart, Lord, thank You for this blessed, uneventful, totally ordinary day.

—*Penney Schwab*

LORD, TOO OFTEN I HANG MY JOY ON others. Oh, God, I want my joy and my self-worth to come from You and You alone. I don't want my joy to hinge on human deeds and human opinions, but on Your saving grace, Your work on the Cross, and the power of the empty tomb. I praise You that You are the source of true joy and true life. Help me to remember this today.

—*Katie Ganshert*

OH, LORD, HOW I WISH I COULD—FOR just one moment—have been among those who were able to see and hear and touch You, even the tassel of Your clothes! Even so, You have graciously caused Your words, the Gospels, to be given to all who would seek them. So I do rejoice, beloved Jesus, in the chance to see and hear and touch and know You through Scripture. I take joy in knowing through Scripture that all of history led to You! I rejoice in experiencing this astonishing truth and in every detail You've provided.

Amen.

—*Marci Alborghetti*

GRANT ME THE GIFT OF KIND WORDS, God. I work to be kind at the office all day, kind to my child's teacher during pick-up time, and kind to my neighbors as I walk into the house. Remind me that my husband, my beloved, deserves the same kindness and not the worn-out bits of me that make it to the couch after the bedtime routine is done. Remind me not to waste spoken words by tainting them with anger, frustration, or exasperation. And grant me the good mind to know when it's time to go to bed!

—*Ashley Kappel*

FATHER, I CONFESS TO BEING TRAPPED by fear and self-pity when I received the doctor's diagnosis. I hung on to worry and gloom. And in my darkness, You saw the anger and resentment that threatened to bring despair. But I thank You that You know the plight of the blind, the sorrow of the poor, the cries of the sick, and the longings of the lonely. I praise You because You shined the light of Your Word to guide my path. You brushed Your love to soothe my heart, and You whispered Your promises for me to rejoice, to trust, and to count on You for my perfect healing. In Jesus's name, I thank You.

Amen.

—*Janet Perez Eckles*

LORD,

I pray for those in ministry today, chosen men and women with a special call to do the work of Your kingdom. Put Your protection on each one. Be their shield from the onslaught of the evil one. Protect their hearts. Defend their morality. Keep them pure and make their hearts tender toward You.

Give them wisdom today as they face the varied needs of those they serve. Fortify them to do what You say is right in an increasingly hostile world. May the Gospel of grace sound forth mightily from their lips and their lives. And may they see the fruits of their ministry in lives changed for Your kingdom forever.

Silence the needless criticisms. Bring harmony and peace to their work. Grant that they do their labor with great joy. Let them labor in a strength from above, in the mighty power of Your Spirit.

Do a special work in their families, Lord. May their spouses feel part of their work, and love You with a great love. May their children never resent You for calling their parents into kingdom work. Provide Sabbath rest for them. Provide financial assistance to them. Provide an extra dose of integrity and character to them. And let the people see Jesus in their ministries and their lives, and bless them for it.

In Christ's grace, amen.

—*Bill Giovannetti*

I'M AFRAID, LORD. AFRAID I WON'T HAVE enough. Afraid of trouble overtaking me. Afraid I'm not good enough. Afraid I will disappoint You or others and be left loveless. I know all of these fears are baseless and false. Instead of fear, let me be flooded with divine reassurance and the truth of Your love for me.

—*Sharon Foster*

FATHER, THANK YOU. YOU ARE THE NAME above all names. You are greatly to be praised. You are my Master. My Savior. My Redeemer. My Deliverer. You are my All in All. You are the One true God. You are Righteous. You are the Alpha and the Omega. You are most definitely more than enough for me.

—*Julie Garmon*

LORD, PLEASE WAKE UP THE DREAMS within me—the ones that You have placed in my heart. The deep desires to do mighty things, to accomplish great conquests, to touch people's hearts with Your love. Show me how to fan into flames the gifts that You've given me. Reveal to me ways I can build and strengthen the core of who I am with the qualities of Who You are, so that together we can change the world, one person at a time. In Your name I pray, amen.

—*Rebecca Ondov*

GOD, I'VE TRIED ALL SORTS OF WAYS TO please You, but I read in Micah 6:8 what it is that You really want from me. Your wish is that I live a changed life—follow a higher calling. You want me to be fair with my words and actions. You yearn for me to readily and easily forgive. Your goal for my life is to show loving-kindness to all I meet. You long for me to feel compassion in every circumstance. Your expectation for my life is modest living. Lord, let me open myself and be vulnerable enough to welcome Your transforming love in my heart so that I might act justly, love mercifully, and walk humbly with You.

—*Stephanie Thompson*

I MISS THEM, JESUS —THESE LIVES THAT brought me joy. You have promised those who love You, "I go to prepare a place for You" (John 14:2, NAS). I have a home, a familiar place waiting—readied for me—where You welcome me. Thank You for explaining this…because every time I think of my beloved ones in the place prepared for them, missing them becomes a little less familiar.

—*Carol Knapp*

THANK YOU, LORD, FOR LOVING ME when I can be so unlovable. You see beyond my moodiness, my complaining, and my tantrums! You see the child You created and You hold me close to Your heart. Help me to love others as You love me.

—*Karen Valentin*

FATHER, GIVE ME SOMETHING TO LAUGH about today. Thank You for creating laughter as a delightful response to the unexpected. May my laughter communicate to You the outlandish difference between my elevated opinions of myself and my human tendencies to bungle and stumble and make messes. Enable me to handle all of my ungraceful moments with good humor. May I delight in the cute and crazy antics of pets and babies. May I uncomplainingly allow my hair to be redone into a surprising new style by the wind. May I skip and sing funny songs and laugh with joy with friends. Thank You for the gift of laughter! I delight in You, oh, Lord. Amen.

—*Karen Barber*

PLEASE MAKE ME BE OPEN TO THE BLESSING in every moment, God. I don't want to miss anything.

—Rhoda Blecker

I LOOKED IN THE MIRROR TODAY, LORD, and saw my age. It startled me. The face I saw is not the face I hold in my mind or feel in my heart. I've always assumed I had so much time. Now I'm not so sure. The number of my years is in Your hands, but I intensely feel their speed.

I want to retain the vigor of my youth. (Fewer wrinkles would be wonderful too.) Enable me to be the best I can be, but not try to be someone or some age I am not. Establish in me the knowledge that what I see in the mirror is influenced by how I live and who I am inside. Remind me that even age is softened by beauty of heart and soul. Show me the best way to take care of my body, for it is Your temple, but work in me so I care more about my character than how I look.

May I never forget that age is a privilege and a gift. Thank You for the growing wisdom and peace my years are bringing. Direct my focus to the joys of my age, for there are many. Teach me to delight in every stage of life. Open my eyes and those of others wide enough to see past my signs of physical aging and appreciate the richness and personal integrity that my years have brought me through Your grace. Help me remember that no matter how many years You grant me on this earth, they are but an eye-blink in the eternity I'll spend with You.

Amen.

—*Kim Henry*

DEAR FATHER, I OFTEN GIVE LIP SERVICE to thanking You for my good health. But today I am really thinking of it. I can go for a walk without a cane. I can eat a healthy diet without restriction. I can breathe without obstruction. It is a gift to have good health. Thank You for making our amazing and wonderful bodies.

Amen.

—*Lisa Bogart*

"SHARE EACH OTHER'S TROUBLES AND problems, and so obey our Lord's 'command'" (Galatians 6:2, TLB). I struggle with this Scripture. Sometimes I get tired of listening…and other times I'm not sure whether or how to help. Holy Spirit, give me discernment! Help me hear with understanding and respond with compassion. Above all, let me resist the temptation to offer unsolicited advice.

—*Penney Schwab*

FATHER GOD, THANK YOU BECAUSE while situations in my life may surprise me, they never surprise You. You know all things. You are never caught off guard. You never sleep or grow weary. When fear of the unknown paralyzes me, help me to rest in the powerful truth that from before the beginning of time, You knew this would happen and even in this, You have good for me.

—*Katie Ganshert*

MERCIFUL GOD, OVER AND OVER AGAIN throughout history, Your people have returned to You, first in humility and repentance, and then, in Your due time, rejoicing. I rejoice in Your limitless Spirit and mercy! It is an extraordinary joy to me that You can and do welcome me back to You whenever I come to my senses and return my heart and mind to Your service. How can You do this, Lord? How do You do it for me, and how do You do it for this shaken world? And yet, You do, because You are God, the One, the Merciful, the Forgiving, the Almighty! I cannot fathom You, Lord, and that makes me rejoice all the more!

Amen.

—*Marci Alborghetti*

THANK YOU, GOD, FOR THE GORGEOUS views looking out the window above my desk at work. I'm blessed to have an office to come to each morning and work that needs my attention. It's a joy to do it— even the cumbersome tasks—when I can admire the beauty of Your world outside the window.

—*Ashley Kappel*

FATHER, THANK YOU FOR GIVING US Your Word to rely on and trust when newspapers relate bad news, when the economy threatens chaos, and the future predicts gloom. What comfort that brings to my soul, knowing that, above all the mess, You're in control. And because You declared victory, we can echo Your good news that wipes away our fears. Confidently, we proclaim Your goodness in the midst of bad times. We speak of Your faithfulness when we're faithless. We stand on the power of Your Word that assures restoration, provision, and a future that's rich with Your compassion and grace. In Jesus's name, amen.

—*Janet Perez Eckles*

PRECIOUS LORD,

I'm thinking of Your Son today, and the day He died for me. I can't begin to imagine the Cross. The agony of the nails and the crown of thorns. The humiliation of His nakedness and beatings. And that awful moment when He cried, "My God, my God! Why have You forsaken me?" How I praise You for the old rugged Cross!

Thank You, Jesus, for bearing my sins. Thank You for paying the price. Thank You for dying for me. Thank You for taking my place. And thank You for the best words ever uttered on planet earth: "It is finished!"

I call You Savior. I call You Risen King. I call You Friend. There is no one like You.

There is no one other than You. I bless Your holy name.

And I am amazed at Your grace. Help me share Your love with someone I see today.

Amen.

—*Bill Giovannetti*

LORD, I STILL MISS MY DADDY AND MY mama. Bless those who have lost loved ones. Let us rejoice in the memories and in the time we held them close. Thank You, Lord, for the hope and eternal life that lies before us.

—*Sharon Foster*

LORD, WHEN LIFE DOESN'T MAKE SENSE, You're never confused. Nothing trips You. You never panic. You hold me in Your righteous right hand. And You'll never, no, not ever, forget me. My name is written in the Lamb's Book of Life, and I am inscribed in the very palms of Your hands. I. Am. Yours.

—*Julie Garmon*

GOOD MORNING, LORD. THANK YOU FOR the gift of another day. Help me to realize that although some days may seem to drag on forever, my life is but a vapor. Teach me how to cherish each moment and how to invest it so that when I come to the end of my days on earth, I won't have regrets, but instead I'll be fulfilled because I've chosen a path that honors You. In Your name, amen.

—*Rebecca Ondov*

LORD, HELP ME TO FIND JOY IN MY DAILY routine. I've been living from alarm clock to alarm clock lately. Work. Chores. Errands. Meals. Bedtime. I'm stumbling through my days with little awareness of how blessed I really am! Show me the joy of everyday living. Better yet, let me bring joy to others today as I work, complete chores, run errands, and eat meals.

—*Stephanie Thompson*

WHAT A SURPRISE! WHEN I THINK OF all the ways to serve You, Jesus, I discover Romans 14:17 (NAS), and learn You are served by "righteousness and peace and joy in the Holy Spirit." Don't I have to be doing something? These seem more like a way of being. Ah, now I get it...a way of being like You.

—*Carol Knapp*

THANK YOU FOR BEING THE STORM OVER
me, Lord. I cried out in despair, but I never
knew it was You, washing things and making
them new.

—*Karen Valentin*

LORD, HELP ME TO LEARN HOW TO GLORIFY You. Glorify isn't something I really know how to do. Please show me how. Let me open myself up to Your glory by seeking the mysterious and beautiful masterpieces of creation that bear the unmistakable mark of You, the Master of Creation. I will mediate upon Your works until I lose myself in wonder and feel compelled to exclaim, "You are the great and glorious God and there is none like You!" And as I return back to my daily life, may others see Your glory reflected in my spirit that has been burnished by my time in Your beaming presence.

Amen.

—*Karen Barber*

HELP ME SEE THE BEAUTY IN EVERYONE and everything. I know You are the source of that beauty, and if I can see it, I can recognize a bit of Your grandeur.

—*Rhoda Blecker*

Lord God, I'm coming to You boldly today. You say in Your Word that whoever asks will receive; and whoever seeks will find; and whoever knocks, the door will be opened. So here I am, Lord, asking. You know my heart and You know my desires. You know them even better than I know them. I lay them before You and ask that You would move mountains. As I wait, help me to trust that no matter what happens, Your ways are best.

—*Katie Ganshert*

BLESSED GOD, I REJOICE IN THE conversion of the hearts of those I love, those I do not love, and those I do not know. Let me be an instrument of their conversion to You, Lord, even as the people of Israel, in their repentance and return to You, were an instrument of conversion to their conquerors. Yet even when I am not a converting influence, I still rejoice in Your Almighty power to turn the hearts and minds of those You chose unto Yourself. Oh, God, who can know Your purpose and Your power? I am overjoyed just to be a witness to the ways in which You draw all things unto Yourself.

Amen.

—*Marci Alborghetti*

FATHER, I CONFESS THAT WORRY FILLS my head more often each day. I have been a fool to seek You only when troubles come, when challenges show up, or gloom threatens to step in. It was only when worry robbed my sleep that I turned to You. I ask that You give me wisdom to choose thoughts of hope, of trust in You, and of confidence because of Who You are. I ask for strength to battle thoughts that usher in worry, anxiety, and fear. I stand on the power of Your Word that declares You've not given me a spirit of fear, worry, or stress. Instead, You gave me the spirit of power, of love, and of a sound mind. A sound mind to know that with You by my side, worry will not come near. In Jesus's name, amen.

—*Janet Perez Eckles*

GOD OF ALL WISDOM,

I come to You for guidance today. I cannot see tomorrow. But I can see You, Who holds tomorrow in the palm of Your hand. Guide my steps today. In the choices I make, the options I face, and the course of life I choose, may I be led into Your perfect will.

By Your grace, may my choices be biblical—never veering from the wisdom of Your Word. By Your grace, may each decision be honest—letting my yes be yes, and my no be no. By Your grace, may each selection among options be wise—doing what is healthy in my life, best for those I love, and, above all, pleasing to You.

I will not go my own way. I will not be wise in my own eyes.

I will trust in You, looking to You to show me the way. Whatever path I choose, I believe with all my heart that You will never leave me or forsake me. For this, I give You praise.

In Christ, amen.

—*Bill Giovannetti*

ONE FOOT IN FRONT OF THE OTHER. THE end prize seems so far away. The journey to the end prize is one foot in front of the other. Help me to enjoy, and see the wonder of, each step. Help me, Lord, to see in the process the sweetness and the beauty.

—*Sharon Foster*

LORD, FORGIVE ME. I HAVE MY EYES ON myself today. When that happens, I believe all sorts of lies, like I'm not smart enough to handle this job. But Psalm 139:14 (ESV) says, "I am fearfully and wonderfully made. Wonderful are Your works; my soul knows it very well." You made me. You understand me. You equip me. And because of these truths, I can handle what You've put before me today and every day.

—*Julie Garmon*

GOOD MORNING, LORD. TODAY I WANT to know You in a more intimate way. As a child of Yours I look at the miraculous works of Your hands and I'm in awe. You created the earth for us to enjoy. The mere fact that Your whole goal was to walk by our side in the Garden of Eden boggles my mind. Today, Lord, help me live up to the desire of Your heart, to walk with You as my constant companion and best friend. In Your name, amen.

—*Rebecca Ondov*

FATHER, WHY IS IT SO EASY FOR ME TO lash out at those I love? Why do I say hurtful things to the people closest to me? It's like my tongue has a mind of its own—when my mouth's engaged, my brain stops! Once spoken, those words get a life of their own. They can travel to others and cause deep pain. Words can exist for a lifetime in the memory of another person, often long after I've forgotten what I've said. Lord, make me mindful of the things I say. Let my words bring life to others today. All my words.

—*Stephanie Thompson*

How is it, Heavenly Father, that on a northern winter day in the thick of January when I faced many unanswered questions, You set a robin in the crabapple tree, when the robin should not have been there at all. It should have been hunkered in warmer climes. Was it a reminder not to worry—that You care for the birds, and I am "worth much more than they?" (Matthew 6:26, NAS).

—*Carol Knapp*

FATHER, I FEEL THAT MY PRAYER LIFE needs strengthening. I'd like to improve both the quality of my prayer times and the quantity of time I spend praying. You know the busy life I lead. So please accept this small conversation as my first step. During the day make me aware of overlooked pockets of time where prayer could thrive if I make the effort to plant it. Help me set aside my long lists of needs and wants so I'll have time to ask You what You want. Show me unique ways that You and I can spend quality time together, enjoying each other's company. Fill me with songs of joy and promises of hope from the Bible. May there be streams of life-giving water flowing through me as my prayer time transforms me into a conduit of Your love, flowing out into a hurting world.

Amen.

—*Karen Barber*

No matter how many times I have witnessed it, Lord, I still struggle to believe my eyes. Once again the frozen, gray corpse of the earth has become as bright and colorful as a box of crayons. Where did You find all these green leaves? These golden daffodils? These white clouds that waltz across an azure sky? And all these baby-blue robins, splashing in April puddles and chasing worms like they were candy?

Father, You sure knew what You were doing when You made spring. And yet, it's frustrating. April is "the cruelest month," as T. S. Eliot wrote. Yes, the air is warm, but the soil is too hard for me to plant my tomatoes. I have cleaned and oiled my fishing rod, but the pond still has a thin crust of ice on it. Those pink dogwoods I planted last spring didn't make it through this hard winter, and I was so hopeful.

For some reason, Lord, I get a bit blue in the spring. Maybe it's because everything in nature is coming to life, but I am still the same old me—a year older, with more aches and pains. The air is warm, but there is a chill in my heart from failing You, yet again. I just seem to blunder my way toward heaven. The sun is glorious, but there are shadows over my future.

Lord, do for me what You have done for the earth. Renew me, and fill me with heavenly happiness.

—*Daniel Schantz*